The Father, The Son,
& The Brother's Ghost

The Father, The Son, & The Brother's Ghost

Twenty Years Gone:
Revisiting a Tragedy and a Trilogy

by John Wayne Samples

2Close2TheGround Publishing
Noblesville, Indiana
Printed in the USA

ISBN-10: 0-61583-715-8
ISBN-13: 978-0-61583-715-4

The Father, The Son, and The Brother's Ghost
Twenty Years Gone: Revisiting a Tragedy and a Trilogy

© John R. Powers & Signet Books

Preface

When my 41-year-old brother died in 1993 I had no idea what to expect for the next 20 days, much less the next 20 years. A lot of people tried to help by giving us books, articles, little speeches, advice and lessons from their own experiences.

Within all that storm of emotion and information my then-supervisor offered me a nondescript little book called *The Junk-Drawer Corner-Store Front-Porch Blues*. I decided to read it because she said it was funny, and because it looked like an easy read that could take me away from the sorrow, rather than immerse me in it.

Page 128 of that book took me by surprise and by anger and by tears and by everything I was trying to avoid. It changed my expectations, or maybe it just gave me some. I never saw the story twist coming and I couldn't keep from making the connection to the real-life experience of losing a loved-one with no warning.

But it was just a book of fiction, and within a day or two I finished it and passed it along to my father with no hint of what was to come.

A couple of weeks later I was at a resort in Wisconsin Dells, wishing I was home with my family. I was there for a conference of the National Rural Electric Association and I had already skipped the previous evening's opening session, preferring to wallow in my grief and lonely hotel room. I had every intention of skipping the morning session, too; it was supposed to start in about an hour. Feeling a little guilty I dug into the registration packet to find the program and read the description of the session I wasn't going to attend.

The keynote was being delivered by a professional speaker named John R. Powers, and the packet contained a list of his accomplishments so we would know he was worth listening to. He did have an interesting bio, including having done some theatrical work on Broadway, and authoring a couple of books: *Do Black Patent Leather Shoes Really Reflect Up?* and *The Junk-Drawer Corner-Store Front-Porch Blues.* I read a few more items on the list before doing the proverbial double take...

The Junk-Drawer Corner-Store Front-Porch Blues!

I showered and dressed in about six minutes, all the time plotting how I was going to meet this guy. I had something to ask him that I knew was going to make things better; he was going to help me understand life and death in a way that could help me get on with either of those directions.

I was sure of it.

Getting to the meeting hall about twenty minutes until start time, I decided my odds of a private conversation were better before the session than afterward when there would be lots of people with questions and maybe even requests to sign books. I scoped out the entrances and exits and chose the door I thought most likely to be the one a person with even a modicum amount of celebrity might use to slip into the conference area. I posted myself about halfway down the hallway so as not to seem too eager, while protecting myself against someone else—like maybe the event coordinator or the AV guy with the wireless mic—getting to him first.

In hindsight, yes, it seems I was laying in ambush.

Less than a minute after I casually leaned against the

wall acting like I was reading a newspaper, the door at the outside end of the corridor opened and in walked John R. Powers by himself.

My greeting probably sounded like I was the official welcoming committee, although I did not intend that misdirection. But knowing he needed to get to the real welcomers, I got right to the point.

"Good morning, Mr. Powers." I introduced myself with a handshake and continued right on. "I need to ask you a question before we go in to the session. About your book..." He was now in polite mode, figuring out quickly that I was not whom he first thought I was. "Please..." he encouraged me to continue.

"I know your *Junk Drawer* book is supposed to be fictional, but Page 128, where one of the brothers leaves the house for a quick run to the store..." my pause is not planned, and he now seems genuinely invested in my question and whatever is behind it.

"The things you wrote in those next few pages, the words you used and the emotions you conveyed, you can't make that stuff up... can you?"

He asked me about my story, about what had happened in my life to make this question so important. He didn't add, "...so important that you would corral me right before my presentation," but I was already beginning to realize how rude and insensitive I was being.

I quickly gave him the basics, including telling him about a recent conversation with my father in which I had told him that it was time 'to get on with our lives' since my brother had now been dead a month already. We needed to move on, and I thought it was my job to get the family moving forward, again.

"So..." this was the question I needed to ask, "was the story of the brother dying in your book real, did it really happen to you? And how long did it take to move on; to get it behind you?"

John's face had been transitioning from glad-to-meet-you to irritated to interested, and now to an expression I couldn't read. What I saw were tears in both eyes.

"It will be 20 years tomorrow." He said it with a half-smile. "It didn't happen the way I wrote about in the book, but it was just as sudden and unexpected." He paused, and I knew if I tried to talk that I would start sobbing, not only because of my own hurt but because of his, and even because of the fictional character in the book that had to carry on without his brother who never returned.

He shifted his briefcase from one hand to the other without taking his eyes from mine.

"And I have not moved on; I can't get it behind me. But I write about it in various ways, using what I felt and what I learned and hoping that it helps someone else to cope with similar loss."

I had no idea what to say or do. John didn't let the moment get uncomfortable, at least not more than it had already become. "Can I sign that?" he was pointing to my copy of *The Junk-Drawer Corner-Store Front-Porch Blues* that I had forgotten I was carrying. I handed it to him without a word. He opened the front cover and wrote, "To John, a new friend with which I share more than just a first name." He closed it and handed it back.

As I was squeezing out a quiet 'thank you' the real welcomers showed up. He smiled once more at me, then went in and wowed the audience with his stories of musicals and families and winning and losing and persevering.

I watched and laughed from just inside the back door, then left quickly when he was through so as to avoid the friends and peers that I feared would want to talk about the presentation and maybe even my brother. I retreated to my room and cried.

Then I got up and wrote a few words, some of which were the beginnings of this trilogy of grief and celebration.

A few weeks later I sent some of my writings to Mr. Powers. He did not invite me to do that so I really didn't expect anything, much less that he might actually read them. But I felt compelled to share them, nonetheless.

Drafts of all three of the stories in this 'trilogy' were included in that package; I sent them via registered mail just so I would at least know that he received them.

The next week I was in another state at another conference. When I checked in with my wife back home during one of the breaks, she tells me "...some guy named John Powers has called for you a couple of times." I got his number from her and called him back immediately from the lobby pay phone.

My egotistical self was just sure that he had shared my writings with his agent and had already negotiated a publishing deal for me. Of course, that was not why he had called.

"John, I've been reading the things you sent me and I want to encourage you to pursue your writing." We talked for a couple of minutes and he gave some specific examples of things he really liked and that he thought had some potential.

I expressed my genuine gratitude that he would even read my stuff, much less call me personally to talk about it. Twice, no less.

This is not to say that John Powers has endorsed this book or anything else I've written. It doesn't mean that the stories are any good or that I am even a decent wordsmith. Those are not among the reasons I'm sharing this story.

But a best-selling author, Emmy-winning TV writer, award-winning musical lyricist, and general gentleman of the craft took a few moments that he didn't have to give, and encouraged a young man in the midst of his grief and his struggles to begin some healing through creative expressions of that grief. I thought that was worth mentioning.

And, I suspect I'm not the only one that can claim that sort of encounter with him.

Since I was first encouraged by John Powers, my writings have been published in multiple magazines, trade & faith publications, and in more recent years in web content, but none of my work has ever seen a printing press in book form. Until now.

Part of my hope in putting these thoughts, adventures and emotions to paper is that someone else may be encouraged by the commonalities of how we muddle through losing someone when it's not yet supposed to be their turn.

While the memories that are rekindled will be unique to each friend and family, the desire to move on will always conflict with the need to stay and reflect in the moment. The need to breathe will always prevail over the gravitational pull toward total silence. And the idea to write a book to teach others how to deal with their grief will either be forgotten, or you will do it. Either way, that hole in your heart will stay with you. And that's okay.

Knowing that you are not the first person, nor will you

be the last, to have no idea what it is you are supposed to do next—or what it was you were supposed to have done then—might bring you a little peace, if not patience.

Life does go on. Laughter doesn't die. Loneliness cries less as you go along, and will eventually stop dominating the conversation.

As my Granny Samples used to say, it's all part of the cycle of life; people have been surviving it for thousands of years, and I bet you will, too.

As I was putting the finishing touches on these pages I thought back to that 'chance' meeting with John Powers, the subsequent phone call, and the encouragement I received from him in just knowing that there were at least two of us who struggled in similar fashion. I decided to look him up to let him know that even though it took twenty years, I'm finally publishing a book (short though it is) and that three or four 'real' books are also in the pipeline and coming soon.

It would be nice if I could tell him those things, and to know that I still think of him when I write. Maybe I'd even sign a copy of this first effort and send it to him in a simple gesture of appreciation.

So, I 'googled' his name in search of a phone number or some other way to reach him.

Instead of finding his number, I found his obituary. John R. Powers died at the age of 67 in early 2013, about the same time I started working on some twentieth anniversary projects to mark the death of my parents' other son. The emotion I felt in a new rush of grief surprised me.

It seems John passed away suddenly and unexpectedly, just like our brothers.

Dr. A. Dain Samples at age 41

Acknowledgments

Granny 'Bear' Samples for saying I could

John R. Powers for calling to say I should

My wife Bobbi for always saying I would

Dedication

To Dain, who did

For the Mother of my Brother
on her 80th Birthday

Mad at Dad

- Have you ever been mad at your father?
- Did you express it or just keep it bottled-up inside?
- Did you feel guilty about it?

I am not a psychologist of any sort, but I was recently faced with these questions when a co-worker whose husband was going through a tough time of unemployment asked me if I had ever been mad at God.

The stresses they were experiencing were threatening their marriage as well as their faith.

The connection may not be obvious, but the first of these stories is the result of that complicatedly simple conversation...

I can only remember two things I was ever angry at my dad about. There were probably more, but only these two remain in my conscious.

The first was when I was about eight or nine years old. I wanted a pony so bad I couldn't stand it and none of Dad's reasons against my desires made any sense. At least I assume they didn't—as I think back now I can't remember him giving me any.

Just no.

A lot of my friends had ponies and I thought I really deserved one. Much later I found out 'why' there was no equestrian surprise under the Christmas tree. Things like our financial situation at the time, the problems in dealing with horses where we lived, and so forth. I still did not like not having a pony, but I was fortunate to have eventually learned some of the reasons why it didn't happen for me.

Then there was the motorcycle. From the time I first saw an old Indian Chief Black Hawk on TV, I wanted one, and I forgot all about the pony.

It didn't help that a missionary friend that was living with us had been given a brand new Honda 90cc Trail Bike for him to take to Africa.

It wasn't a Black Hawk, but it was real and I could touch it. At night it would just sit there in our garage under my bedroom and call my name.

Every now and then my brother and I would get to ride it around the yard, and I even got pretty good at zigging and zagging on it through the tombstones in the church cemetery next door.

But that was the missionary's ride. I needed my own, and something more like a 175cc!

The better I got on that Trail Bike, the hotter the burning in my soul. As a teenager I was prepared and able to get a job to pay for it myself, so I knew I had Dad behind the proverbial eight-ball when the time came to get his permission to purchase.

Among the reasons for my soon-to-be-in-the-saddle confidence was our basic transportation needs due to our rural home being so far from school and all my friends. "You wouldn't have to take me everywhere... I would have my own ride," was one of the lines I'd been practicing.

But the biggest trump card I had was knowing that I was the 'good son' that had already and repeatedly demonstrated dependability, even as my brother, almost four years older than me, would stretch the

boundaries of respect and behavior.

Dad just couldn't say no to me.

But he did.

Just no.

For weeks and months.

Just no.

As my anger over this futile journey into manhood began to invade the rest of my relationship with my father, I decided to force the issue.

Dad was driving me someplace he wouldn't have to be driving me if only I had that bike, so the time was perfect.

With a voice that was probably not quivering as much as my memory suggests, and palms that were curiously reminiscent of the sweaty sensation I experienced the first time I asked a girl on a real date, I notified him that I *was* going to get a "bike", and since he really hadn't given me any good reasons why I shouldn't, he couldn't stop me.

The silence was deafening for about a minute. Then, when he took his eyes off the road just long enough

to look right into my heart, I saw the glint of at least one tear.

For reasons I still don't understand, I remember that it was 3:34 on an early April afternoon. I remember that we were right in front of Mike and Gary Harrison's house, two brothers about my age that were going to be impressed with my new wheels. And I remember exactly what he said:

> *"John Wayne, I want you to have that*
> *motorcycle so badly I can hardly stand it.*
> *I can't really tell you why I won't let you have*
> *it, except there's just something inside me*
> *telling me it's the wrong thing to do."*

I never gave the rest of my prepared remarks. To this day that remains the most powerful "just no" he ever gave me about anything.

I still didn't understand.

I still didn't agree.

I still was angry.

But I became suddenly aware of a trust in my father's judgment which I never realized before.

Two weeks later my brother was out pushing the boundaries on the missionary's motorcycle and ended up being involved in a rather serious accident while riding on the rural road that ran by our house.

Without Dad's permission.

My brother was bloodied and bruised, but otherwise okay.

I, on the other hand, had just lost any chance I had of winning on appeal. Case closed.

So, what's the point?

Where's the connection?

These memories first haunted me several years ago while struggling through my own extended period of unemployment and related marital problems.

I had never allowed myself to be mad at God before. It just seemed like some kind of unforgivable sin and I just wasn't going to do it.

Then one day I couldn't hold back anymore. I let loose verbally and loudly and angrily and tearfully

and frightfully and specifically at God. I still don't know if it was the "right" thing or not, I just know that it happened. I suspect it also happened with Moses and some of the other prophets.

Perhaps even the apostles as they wrestled with the reality they could see between the crucifixion and the resurrection.

And maybe even Christ in the Garden.

What I do know is that the day I let loose on God, my relationship with Him was profoundly and positively affected in a way that has completely changed how I think, worship, communicate and seek to serve. Whether I'm justified or completely out of line, knowing that I can be emotionally honest with God and not be struck down by a bolt of lightning has been an on-going revelation to me.

The connection to the memories of being genuinely and openly in disagreement with my earthly father are clear to me and very strong.

Anger is not something to seek out or to express lightly or on a whim. But it can also be very real and can get in the way of our worship, especially when we deny it by acting like everything's all right while we pray or commune.

If God knows our love, then He also knows our anger.

I don't think we are ever at risk in our relationship with the Almighty because of our natural emotions, but when those emotions dictate our behavior, or lack of it, it is reasonable to expect relational impact, and maybe even a time of being held accountable.

The first time I got mad at God, He blessed me in such a way as to say, "I'm going to show you 'why' *this time*, but next time you've got to trust Me."

I felt very fortunate to have been shown, but also felt a certain shame. Not shame that I had expressed my anger, but that I had expressed my lack of vision and trust.

I still get mad at God. I doubt that I've ever been justified in my complaints and demands, but I don't think I've been wrong in expressing them.

I wish I did not wrestle with this, and it still doesn't feel right, but it is a real—if infrequent—part of my relationship with Him.

Just like it is with my dad.

Mad at Dad was first written in late March, 1993. I shared a copy of it with my father in early April.

Two weeks later my brother died very unexpectedly while teaching a class at the University of Cincinnati. He left behind a blossoming career, heart-broken parents, a frightened wife, 14-month-old twin boys, and a brother who desperately needed another connection to help it all make sense.

While I'm still hoping to find a reason for this loss, I realize we may never know the whys of our grief.

Will understanding that we may never know be enough to keep away the anger?

Probably not.

But I also know, based on all my experience, that the Father is faithful.

In His time. In His way.

And sometimes that just makes me so mad I can hardly stand it ...

The End

The Father, The Son, & The Brother's Ghost

Up the Road a Piece
an embellished recollection

The clock on the dashboard reads 5:55. The country station agrees with that just before I hit the seek button in search of the baseball game that's supposed to be about to start.

It's a warm April afternoon on Interstate 80 in the middle of Iowa. A sudden illness in the family has caused me to cut short a business trip in Nebraska and head for Cincinnati where I'll meet up with my wife and kids and relatives and friends.

I'm already tired and wishing I had someone to ride with me. I even pray one of those quick *just in case He's listening* prayers for some divine intervention to help me stay awake. Right now I'd settle for a cup of caffeine.

The billboard claims there's free coffee at the next exit—eight more miles. I'm wondering how much

"free" will cost when I'm struck by the sight of a happy-go-lucky low-risk-looking hitchhiker.

Ask and ye shall receive, I think to myself as I slow down to look for signs of drugs or accomplices. He's carrying nothing and I can see for three states in all directions so I figure he's safe. As I pull to a stop, I'm wondering where his car is and how he got out here.

   "Where ya headed?"

As I listen for his response, I'm thinking that I haven't heard that line in a long time, at least not through the passenger-side window of a car driven by a pity-taking good Samaritan.

But there was a day when "Where ya headed?" was the calling card of the fortunate who were willing to share some of their success with poor travelers trying to make their way on worn-out soles and an outstretched thumb. Soldiers. Sailors. Students. All getting rolling glimpses of people and vehicles as they evaluated the behavior and attitude of each—the drivers and the cars. You can learn a lot between here and the next town about a worn-out soul trying to make way on four new tires and an outstretched hand. Businessmen. Farmers. Lonely Women.

I always got the businessmen and farmers, but it was the stories of the Lonely Women, the tales told and the hopes of fantasies fulfilled, that gave strength to the thumb and comfort to the feet. That is what made hitching worth all those risks: the crazed, gun-toting mass-murderer; the old guy with a Sears and Roebuck drivers license; or Rod Serling in the back seat saying something about, "... two people unaware of what lies ahead, on the road to the Twilight Zone."

I always thought Lonely Women caused more guys to hitch than all the flat tires and empty gas tanks combined.

> *"Just up the road a piece," he drawls back in perfect time.*

It was like the coded exchange between secret agents.

"... up the road a piece" meant there was no crisis, nothing to fix or fill-up, and that you were an experienced rider who would probably even make good conversation for as long as you were in the car. It might mean a mile, or it might mean 30 miles. It might mean 'till it's just time to get out.

My brother and I were teenage thumb travelers. He would hitch the 20 miles between our rural home and his high school. It was the only way he could participate in those well-rounding types of extra-curricular activities which help a person get a better education which helps a person get a better job which helps a person afford a car so he can be the driver instead of the rider.

In contrast, I would just go up the road a piece to Wesley Johnson's place for a game of kill-or-be-kilt wiffle ball. But I might stop at Jeff Barnes' for basketball—if I didn't see Mike Roberts there first. Or I might get out at Sid Martin's store at the crossroads for an RC Cola and a Moon Pie if the feeling so struck. The driver had to be flexible.

The only variable my brother had in his travel itinerary was he would sometimes stop off at the old folks home and read to Aunt Hassie (she wasn't really his aunt), or listen to her stories of conquering teachers and teaching conquerors. I'm sure he never used the *up the road a piece* line because he always knew where he was going and wanted everyone to know he knew.

Even if he might change his mind after he got in, he always stated his plans up front because everyone

knowing where they are going has always been important to him.

"Well, jump on in here. That's exactly where I'm headed," I chuckled back knowing that riders would always trust a guy with a sense of humor—especially if they were going to exactly the same place.

He glides into the front seat.

"So, did your car break down or something?" I'm watching an approaching semi in the side mirror wishing he would move to the left lane so I can pull back on to the highway. "I mean, you don't see many hitchhikers on the Interstate anymore unless there's a dysfunctional vehicle around." I pull back on the highway.

"That's a fact." He says it with a grin that I can see without looking. I'm not sure if it is a fact that his car broke down or he is just agreeing about the highway hikers.

Through the static of a radio station not yet ready to be received, Marty Brenneman welcomes us to the pre-game show and begins setting-up tonight's game between the Reds and somebody they're expected to beat but probably won't.

My guest is amazed that I can pick-up the Cincinnati station way out here. Good. He knows the rules. The rider should always find something to compliment about the car. Even a good AM radio. I start to explain that the signal will come in better once the sun has been down a while. "I used to live in Ohio," he volunteers. I realize he isn't impressed with the radio after all, just the station's origination location. "Seems like a lifetime ago that I was there, but it was real good while it lasted."

He still hasn't answered my first question. I decide to be more direct. "So what are you doing out here?"

"Just been travelin' around, looking for questions and answers, not necessarily in that order." Straight face. Ok, so I picked-up an intellectual hippy. That's not dangerous. Is it?

"By the way. I really appreciate you picking me up. Today has been a really hard day. But I'm over it now. Thanks a lot."

He doesn't look like he's had a hard day. I'm not really all that interested in his problems anyway.

But, I am courteous.

"What was so tough about it?" I'm just waiting for

my turn to lay my tough break up against anything he can throw out.

"Kind of odd," he muses. "The last ride I had didn't want to let me out. I've never seen anything like it. I asked them to stop maybe five or six hours ago, but they just kept on going."

OK, so now I'm curious. "You mean they didn't let you out at your stop?"

"Well, there really wasn't a specific stop. Sometimes it's just time to get out, if you know what I mean. It was just time, but they wouldn't stop." He looks like he's half-way between a smirk and a cry. I don't think I believe him. I'll try a new approach.

"So, where you headed now?"

"To tell you the truth, I have a hunch my traveling days are over. Maybe one more stop—just up the road a piece—and I can rest for a while."

I respect the *"just up the road"* line so I back-off. For now.

Marty finishes the expected starting line-ups and begins interviewing some guest with a southern twang about his days in Triple A as a Louisville Red Bird.

I think about a joke my dad used to tell about the Kentucky hitchhiker who only had one shoe. "No, sir," he replied to the driver who asked if he had lost one. "I found one!"

That makes me think about Shoeless Joe Jackson and that makes me wonder if they really did make that **Field of Dreams** movie here in Iowa. That makes me smile out loud; I usually do when I think of that film. I recall that the last time I saw it I was with my brother. And I think it was the first time we ever cried together.

"Ease his pain."

Just for a moment I'm afraid to respond; afraid the voice hadn't come from my passenger. I take the chance. "Did you say something?" That should be safe.

"You know, the place where they filmed that baseball movie. It's just up that road a piece." He points to the approaching exit for State Road 38, and arcs his hand to the left indicating a faraway destination to the north. "Waaayy up that road a piece."

"Is that right?"

I try to act calm as I glance in the rear-view mirror to see if a Mr. Serling is in the back seat.

This guy is acting real cool, like he really hadn't just read my mind. "Yep. Go about seventy-five miles, then turn right when you see that long line of cars." His smile is bigger than his little joke is funny.

"Is that where you're headed?" I expect I'm on to something, finally.

"Heavens no," he puns back. "I've been afraid of cornfields ever since I saw that movie." His smile is genuine but he doesn't milk it. As he turns to look out his window at what will soon be miles upon miles of cornfields, he kind of mumbles. "Always wanted to be a shortstop myself."

Our thoughts drift separately for a few minutes. Maybe an hour. The radio comes in real clear just long enough to reminded us that the home team blew another big lead last night. "Stupid Reds." I don't think he hears me.

"Did you find your answers?"

He heard that. "You know, the ones you've been traveling around looking for?"

"Some, but I think I'm about to find a lot more

where I'm headed today."

"Oh, yeah? Where's that?" Somehow, I don't expect a straight answer.

> *"Just up the road a piece."*

I was right.

The reception is getting worse, not better, so I turn off the radio during the commercial. Answering the question that he never asked, I explain that I'll turn it back on when I get a little closer.

> *"To Cincinnati?"*

I tell him what has happened and that I'm trying to get there before dawn. He doesn't really respond.

For the next couple of miles the only sound is the predictable click of the tires marking time and distance by the newly patched cracks running across the highway. Nice beat, but I don't think I could dance to it. I turn the radio back on and punch in the tape; Paul Simon's Graceland starts to play. My rider wants to know if he can ask me a question. I turn the music down.

> *"What will you do when you get to the hospital in Cincinnati?"*

I tell him that I don't really know. He tells me that he doesn't really know either. So much for traveling around looking for answers.

I turn the music back up.

We both join in on *You Can Call Me Al*. I'm doing the Chevy Chase part from the music video and he's acting like Paul Simon. I'm feeling pretty good by the time the song ends and he says thanks for the ride and it's time to get out.

"But we're fifteen miles between exits," I protest. He says something about taking a side road or two.

I turn off the stereo and pull over. More thanks. I offer him money to ride all the way back to Ohio with me. "Nah," he says. "We've both gotta do what we've gotta do. No since putting it off." He wishes me luck and I return the sentiment, even though I still don't know where he's headed or why he might need luck.

As I'm pulling back onto the highway, watching for semis in the side mirror, I notice he's ... I never asked his name ... I notice he's crossing the median to the west-bound side and sticking his thumb out even before he gets there. I quickly get up to speed and set the cruise control on 72 just as my car

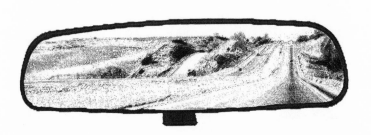

phone rings. It's my wife. She's tried calling a half-dozen times.

No need to hurry; he's gone.

When?

About 30 minutes ago; just before six o'clock.

The surgeons fought hard to keep him alive for the last five or six hours, but when they removed the life support, well, there was just too much damage to my brother's heart.

Professor Alan Dain Samples was 41. Survivors include his wife and fourteen month old twin sons...

In an instant I'm flooded with questions that need immediate answers: Who's going to write the obit? Why should parents ever have to bury their children? Who's going to teach his class tomorrow? Why should children have to grow-up without their dad? When did we last talk and what was it about?

For no rational reason I quickly look up at the rear-view mirror. Nobody there; just a hot highway melting into the last few strands of daylight. Didn't really expect anyone to be there.

I don't think.

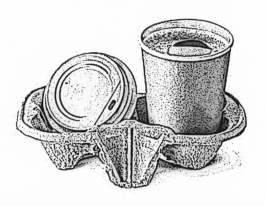

I set the cruise to the speed limit and turn on the headlights. Thankful that the rest of the family can be together during such a tough time, I wonder if I can stay awake for another seven-plus hours.

I decide to stop for a cup of coffee, just up the road a piece.

The End

Catching a Dream

It may be the most absurd thing I have ever done; it may be the most normal. I still don't know.

Sixteen hours of a forty-eight hour weekend on the road.

Nine hundred miles in a mini-pickup truck and two nights in motel rooms with a man more than twenty years my senior.

Our cargo consists of two sets of golf clubs, two cases of cassettes of all our favorite stuff that we want the other one to hear, two overnight bags, two pockets full of money, two hearts still on the mend, two expectations that will never be met, too many things that we don't know how to talk about, and two baseball mitts—one with my initials and the other with those of my son.

I don't remember my father ever having his own glove, but there was always one for him to use, usually that overstuffed flat one like the kinds worn by guys named Ty and Babe and Honus and

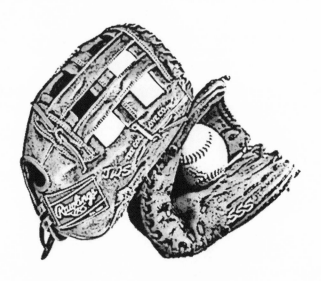

Shoeless and Moonlight back before artificial turf, free agency, and night games at Wrigley Field. Way before the night games!

We also have one baseball, but Dad doesn't know about that, or about the gloves for that matter. They are going to be surprises when we get *there*.

This is Dad's Father's Day gift. Just one of those *We'll-have-a-good-time-then* ideas that we actually followed-through on. One of those father/son bonding things that usually requires some kind of life-changing trauma that makes you spend more time with the people that you should have been spending more time with anyway. One of those things you do after burying your parents' other son and realizing you've become an only child for the first time.

Just one of those things.

This is a pilgrimage. It's a purging. It is a fantasy flight to a foreign feast of unfathomable fun. It's a long ways away.

It's laughing at the Steven Wright tape when he interrupts his own story from four years ago with, "...no, that was yesterday!"

It's crying when the country singer sings about all he would have done differently if he'd only known "...that it was the last time."

It's dancing with our theology as we try to come to terms with a suddenly snuffed-out point of light.

It's flirting with every waitress, no matter what her age or aesthetic value, because that's just what guys do when they're just guys.

We *are* just guys. It's one of the few times we've been just guys since Dad taught me to lure a Tennessee rock bass out of its hiding place in the pond on Dale Haren's 2-BZ-2 Farm twenty-five years ago.

We leave my house in Indianapolis after work on Friday hoping to make it to a "Vacancy" sign in Peoria. No problem. After letting Dad win the fight over who gets to pay for the room, we proceed to the next-door eatery for some midnight ribs, nachos, chicken wings, and miscellaneous other delicacies better left to a different time of day. Just because that's what guys do. The waitress doesn't return our flirts so we dock her tip.

That feels manly.

Before heading out the next morning we check the weather channel on the hotel cable TV. They're predicting a beautiful day where we're headed so we allow our expectations to rise.

An incredible lightning show welcomes us to the land of the Hawkeyes and ushers in the promise of a wet fulfillment to our trek. We are soon engulfed in one of those perpetual, soaking rains that you think may never end.

As we pull into our destination—Dyersville, Iowa — we can't help but wonder how in the world the movie producers found this middle-of-nowhere little burg of four thousand fortunates. The brochure says Dyersville is world famous for farm toys and for a basilica.

We've seen farm toys.

Not sure what makes a church a basilica, we go there—mostly because it represents dryness on a rainy day. But, were it not for what was to come, this could have been the highlight of the trip.

There's a wedding taking place in this worshipful wonder and we become architectural tourists caught in an exchange of nuptials. We are part of the moment as two lives begin sharing one road.

Our tears surprise us both. I tell Dad that it's the little unexpected things that make trips like this great. He agrees.

I'm not sure how we know that since we've never taken a trip like this.

As we leave, it's still raining. We decide to go ahead and drive by our final destination to see if it's even open. If it looks worthwhile, we'll come back to town, kill some time, then go back after the rain stops. The map says it's about three miles out a series of ninety degree turns in the road. That's how I remember the final shot of the movie with all the cars filled with people looking for a dream.

As we crest the last hill and *The Field* rises up before us, I'm expecting some great flood of emotion to overtake me.

There's the top of the lights, then the familiar white house with the red barns. The backstop is right where it's suppose to be and the bleachers are intact. Everything is as expected, except there's no emotional overflow.

Then I notice the souvenir stands; I should have expected that. The house looks a lot closer to *The Field* than it did in the movie. The drowned corn is

not high enough to fade into.

Why am I here?

As we pull into the farm yard to park we have to jockey around to give a couple of other cars room to leave. Why are they here? Why are those guys out on *The Field* in the mud and the rain?

There are more people than I noticed from the road. A quick count finds forty seven souls; three on the diamond, ten huddled under the souvenir stand, a dozen or so just meandering around, several women sitting in cars wondering why they are here, and the rest just standing and watching and taking pictures of the action on *The Field*. Dad and I decide to go for it.

I pull out the surprise gloves and ball and utter the predictable, "Dad, wanna have a catch?" This is it. The emotional flood. The memory we'll never forget. The Kodak moment.

Or not.

"Oh," he understates, "you brought the gloves. Good."

We saunter out to right field.

Another Dad is pitching to another son while the other brother shags the hits in left field. There is no catcher. We position ourselves so we can both see the batter in case he hits our way. He doesn't. I think we're starting to have a pretty good time as we toss and talk and talk and toss.

In the rain.

I'd forgotten how strong Dad's arm was. Just as I start to comment on it, he winces with pain as his curveball wannabe pops my glove. He says nothing, but he starts throwing the ball with a fancy underhand motion. A line comes to mind from the 1968 Bobby Russell song about the neighborhood's favorite dad and hero: *The old major leaguer had to quit 'cause he said he threw his arm away.*

My next throw is wide and right and glances off the top of his glove. I start to apologize when I get smacked by a flashback. "Never, never, never apologize for a bad throw." Dad rarely acted like he was upset with having to chase my errant intentions, but he hated my apologies. "That just makes it easier for you to accept it yourself when you say 'I'm sorry.' Don't be sorry, be on target." I was never sure I understood that, but I was always impressed with the thought process.

By the time he gets back with the ball, I've had enough. He doesn't argue and we head back toward the truck. I realize we need some pictures and tell him to wait by the backstop.

As I'm digging around behind the seat for the camera, I find it. Not the camera, the flood. The emotions. The overflow. It's raining hard enough that people outside can't see in the truck, so I just stand there, bent at the waist with the half of me outside getting rained on, the half of me inside raining on the upholstery. A cleansing sob. A few seconds. Maybe a minute.

Oh yeah, the camera. Dad. He's getting rained on all over.

I tuck the moment-maker under my wet golf shirt and head for the backstop.

A few more dreamers are now shagging flies.The father is still pitching. He laughingly complains that his All-Conference Batting Champion son should swing more so he wouldn't have to retrieve so many balls. I tell Dad to watch the camera as I settle into the catcher's squat behind the plate.

A couple of other guys are putting on their gloves and sloshing out to their favorite positions. The kid

in the box starts hitting balls all over *The Field*. One splashes into the corn, then melts into the mud as it rolls out of view. Everybody cheers. Nobody chases that ball.

Out of the corner of my eye I notice Dad trying to figure out my camera, so I concentrate on striking the best catcher's stance I can, just in case he's successful. Ten or twelve pitches later my knees remember why Johnny Bench retired so early. I call for time so I can get a picture of Dad with the farm house in the background.

As we walk off The Field, a new arrival jumps out of a van almost before it stops. I recognize him from the wedding at the basilica in town. The old brown glove he's wearing doesn't match his tuxedo, but that seems to be the last thing on his mind. He takes my spot behind the plate; one tux tail lays in the mud, the other floats in a puddle.

When I see him a few minutes later at the souvenir stand I have to chuckle at how his tuxedo goes with that wet look, and how sad his patent leathers look trimmed in mud. But his whole image is quickly preempted by his smile which radiates an importance of which he seems to think he has just been a part.

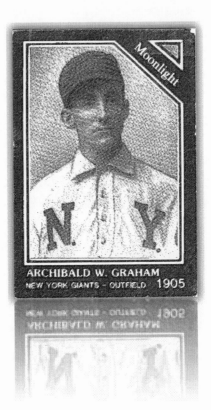

Moonlight

ARCHIBALD W. GRAHAM
NEW YORK GIANTS - OUTFIELD 1905

Several of us standing there begin to wish we were wearing good clothes that could be ruined like his.

It suddenly strikes me that this is really nuts. As Dad and I marvel at the almost constant flow of cars in and out of the farm lot, we ask each other what it is that we share with all these people that makes us risk pneumonia to play an imagined inning of a kid's game on a fantasy field built by Hollywood dream makers?

Dad says it has to do with hope and being a kid again. I suggest that it has to do with wanting another chance to do it right.

Terrance Mann says it's because baseball has been the only constant throughout our history.

Little Karen Kinsella says we don't have any idea why we came. But we all did. She said we would.

A magnet, a coffee mug, a jersey, a Moonlight Graham baseball card, and it's time to go. Should we come back after the weather clears? We agree the mission is complete.

The drive home starts about thirty-three minutes after we arrive. We had planned for a lot more time, but we didn't want to wear out *The Field*.

Or the Dreams.

The rain has somehow made it more memorable, more worthwhile, more bonding with all the other wet heads who didn't have sense to wait for the sun.If it had been a beautiful day, our expectations of the people and the playing and the being may have all been met, but this was better.

Five minutes down the road the rain completely stops. Thirty miles later the sky is blue and the air is filled with that crisp scent of success. It feels absurdly normal.

But then, as every player who's won on the road will tell you, the sun always shines on the way home when you've had a good game.

The End

Appendix

As a further reminder of the person we are remembering in these stories, this section is taken from my brother's official farewell. They include his obituary, some of the remarks made at his memorial service, and ends with a poem. The last section of this book will include some of professor Dain Samples' academic contributions.

A teacher in life, Dain was also a teacher in death as he left his body to the medical school to be used for instructing students.

His memorial service was conducted on April 24, 1993 at the Andersonville Christian Church in Andersonville, Indiana.

The Andersonville Church was the source of some of Dain's earliest memories as his grandfather (Papa Daddy) C.M. Estes, was the minister of the church from the late 1940s to the early 1950s.

In the weeks before his passing, Dain had been talking about those memories and his desire to return to Andersonville for a visit.

The following pages have been transcribed from an audio tape of the memorial service, and documents our family's last visit to Andersonville.

The Obituary

Born Oct. 17, 1951 Alan Dain Samples died unexpectedly Wednesday evening, April 21, 1993 in Cincinnati's University Hospital.

He was currently serving as Assistant Professor at the University of Cincinnati. He was teaching a computer science class when he collapsed with what was later determined to be a spontaneous aortic dissection.

He studied at Indiana University, Milligan College (TN), IUPUI and Purdue University. He Received his Ph.D. in Computer Science from the University of California at Berkeley in 1991.

He attended Boones Creek High School and University High School in Johnson City, Tennessee.

He was a 1969 graduate of Washington High School in Indianapolis.

He is survived by his wife Patricia Ann McColpin Samples; twin sons, Ehren John and Galen Macesten (14 months); parents John C. Samples and Joyce Samples, all of Cincinnati, and one brother, John Wayne Samples (wife Bobbi), of Indianapolis.

The family requests that in lieu of flowers donations be made to:

The A. Dain Samples Memorial Fund
Dept. of Electrical and Computer Engineering
University of Cincinnati, Cincinnati, OH
45221-0030

The Fund will be used for on-going student and teacher awards at the University.

*"If I count every year
I've been in school as a grade,
then I've graduated from the 28th grade."*

--Dr. A. Dain Samples, 1991
on the completion of his doctorate.

*"He sought to understand why people believed
their ideas to be correct, and learned more
from that effort than by trying to
prove them wrong."*

--Dr. A. Dain Samples, 1993
Just days before his death the school newspaper did a profile piece
on this popular new professor. This was his answer to the question,
"What would you want your tombstone to say about you?"

Dain's Day: The Memorial Service

Music

Selections from Dain's favorites, followed by two of his parent's favorites

- Cats In The Cradle / Vincent (Instrumentals)
- Pianist: Steve Roberts, Ocala, Florida
  Dain's Milligan College "roomie" and friend
  of 22 years.
- Send In The Clowns
- Vocalist: Anita Lenas, Interlachen, Florida,
  Dain's sister-in-law.
- Because He Lives (Instrumental)
- How Great Thou Art

Prayer

by Ralph Small, friend of the family.

Greetings by John C. Samples, Dain's father

This is Dain's Day, and we are here to make it his day. Thank you for coming.

Every time I move my eyes I see new people that I am glad to see. On behalf of Dain's wife, Pat, and my wife, Joyce, and myself, Thank you for coming. This is Dain's Day.

I'm pleased to see family, I am thrilled to see friends, I'm honored to see some of Dain's contemporaries and peers, and I am thrilled to see some of Dain's students. You sure help to make this... almost bearable.

Would the students from the University stand, please? (many students stand and are applauded.) Thank you. Thank you very much.

- There are some things I want to call to your attention as we begin our time of tribute together:

- There's some information in the program that will tell you about the Dr. Alan Dain Samples Memorial Fund at the University of Cincinnati.

- Please take opportunity before you leave after the service to come and see some of the things here that speak of Dain's life. There are other things on the table over here... I even see the little bean bags that he used to practice juggling with all the time. You need to see some of those things. We need for you to see some of those things.

- And then, you're invited following the service to follow the convoy over to Lake Santee, which is about 12 to 15 miles south of here, where we will meet in the community center. We'll have some food and we'll have some fellowship and we'll have some memories. For those of you traveling either to Cincinnati or to Indianapolis, you'll not be getting any farther away from your destination because there is an easy route from there over to I-74 to go either way.

And now, our son, John Wayne, has a tribute for his brother.

John W. Samples, Dain's brother

My Dad tells a story of when he was preparing to speak a few years ago. A preacher friend of his looked at his notes and said, "Are you afraid?"

My dad says, "Yes, I am."

His friend said, "If I had to speak from notes like that I'd be afraid, too."

So... *(there is laughter as he holds up two pages of scribbles)*
please bear with me.

I also tried to make this short, then I decided... NOT! (laughter)

Dain, many years ago, was an actor. I loved that about him. I tried to emulate that, and in recent years as I have tried to do it some more, I began to realize the difference between Dain and I is that he was an acTOR, and I was acTING. There is a difference.

Dain has played his final role, and today I am playing my hardest role.

I think Dain would appreciate this service today, because he always loved playing to a packed house.

Speaking of acting, there were three movies... As I'm sorting through this... As I got the news... I spent a long time in a car driving back here from Nebraska on Wednesday so I had a lot of time to do a lot of sorting.

For some reason three movies just kept coming back. They were the first three movies my brother ever took me to see after he got his drivers license. In fact, as I think about it, it may be the only three movies he took me to see. Two of them make sense and the third one I wasn't so sure about:

Romeo & Juliet. Dain loved Shakespeare, and he was a romantic. And he loved Romeo & Juliet.

The Heart is a Lonely Hunter. It was the first time since we were just children that I saw Dain cry. And the first time as a 13 or 14 year old adolescent I considered that perhaps it's okay for teenagers to cry. And every tear that comes out today makes me think of Dain telling me it's okay to do that.

The third one was a little more difficult. Butch Cassidy & the Sundance Kid. (laughter) And I'm thinking, "Why is this significant? Why is this haunting me here today?" I got to the point where I remembered how hard he laughed at the cliff scene. Jumping over the cliff... (laughter) You've seen the movie. He had a wonderful laugh.

And then this morning, as I'm leaving Cincinnati, the raindrops were falling all over the windshield, and I thought, "That's the significance. Raindrops keep falling on our heads."

I never went to Dain for much advice. We had a wonderful relationship, but I just never went to anybody for much. But Dain gave me two pieces of advice as I was growing up and I'm not sure why I remember them. I'm pretty sure he's not the only one that ever gave me these pieces of advice, but he's the only one I remember doing it because he was very specific and pointed. I'm not going to tell you what the situation was, but he got right in my face one day and he says, "John Wayne, you don't put other people down for their ignorance." And a few months later, in a similar situation, he says, "You don't build yourself up at other people's expense."

Those two things have just been so important to me as I've grown up. And it was Dain's unsolicited advice that I credit that to.

And I felt a little guilty [driving back] that my big brother was gone and I really hadn't spent much time seeking his counsel and his advice overtly. Then I realized that there have been three times in my life when I've had life-changing types of trials. The first two times, Dain was the first one I called. But he's not here to call this time.

Dain loved to debate. Is that a surprise to any of you students? He loved to debate. We would debate everything from theology, to which hole to crawl through when we were trying to find our way out of a cave. When you're 300 feet under the ground and you don't know which way to go, those debates can get pretty theological themselves.

There was a time when I thought he just liked to argue for the sake of arguing, then a few years ago I realized, no, *he likes to debate because he learns when he debates*. It wasn't until a few years ago that I realized that winning the debate wasn't even what was terribly important to him. As long as you could convince him he was wrong with empirical evidence, and all those other words he would use. If you could convince him he was wrong and he saw the error of his ways, he enjoyed that. He enjoyed learning so much that losing the debate was secondary.

The last debate we had, and I guess this gets back to the raindrops on the windshield this morning—until just now I hadn't made that connection—the last debate we had was five or six miles down the road from here at the Hearthstone Restaurant down by Metamora last Christmas. We were debating: Does the speed of the car effect how wet the windshield gets? (laughter)

{Bobbi adds, "For an hour and a half!"} (more laughter) For an hour and a half Dain and I were going nose to nose on this and I had it figured out and he had it figured out and after an hour and a half—Bobbi's been sitting over there taking it all in —and she says, "You know, I think you're forgetting this factor." I have forgotten the details now, but she throws that in and I'm going, "Yeah, okay, Bobbi." And Dain goes, "She's right!" He gets out his pencil and his calculator and he starts saying, "She's absolutely right!" And he got all excited. He did not mind being shown he was wrong. He enjoyed it.

Back in Dain's days as a preacher we had theological debates on issues such as once-in-grace-always-in-grace, the necessity of baptism, women's roles in the church—just little things like that. (laughter) In more recent years, our debates have become more... significant. Sometimes more...painful. The debates have been more about essence of life issues as Dain has investigated some different paths.

No matter what the issue was, Dain never hid his opinions from me. He never expected me to hide my opinions from him. And I deduce from that— and many other things—that he was a man of immense integrity. I loved him deeply, and he is one of the few people I have known in my life for which there has never been a question that he loved me. But as many of you know, our views of the hereafter have not been the same for many years. Now, I need to go back to something ...

Dain had a look that I will never forget as long as I live. Whenever he would discover a new truth, and I know you students have seen this look, whenever he had been convinced that he had been wrong, his eyes would open wide, his forehead would disappear into his hairline, he would always do something with his hands, and he would grin this toothy grin that was just infectious.

If I could be so presumptuous today, I'm going to claim victory in our final debate about the afterlife. Because, if I'm right, the last couple of days have seen a lot of reconciliation on the golden streets.

And, my guess is, there's a new grin infecting half of heaven!

Thank you.

John C. Samples, Dain's father

If Dain were here, I would begin by saying... Well, because he would appreciate the humor of it, I would begin by saying, 'Dain was not perfect; he took after his mother's side of the family'. (laughter) Those who know his mother see the obvious humor in that. Or, maybe it's those who know me see the obvious humor in that. (more laughter)

No, he wasn't perfect, but you know, today the flaws are invisible. And as a tribute to Dain, I want you to see him through a proud father's eyes.

Dain was a scholar. I want to share with you some of the things I saw in my son. He was a scholar; always reading. You seldom saw him that he did not have a book, either in his hands, or not more than an arm's length away. It was true from childhood.

One of our favorite family stories is when he found Joyce's book on nursing obstetrics and promptly wanted to know, how did we get in there in the first place? (laughter) He got a direct answer.

Dain was a musician. Taught himself to play. He could play a decent piano; even enjoyed the classics. And he loved all forms of music, except two: country and western. (laughter)

Dain was a thinker. He was a thinker. Something else he learned from his mother's side of the family. I remember in the first grade he heard a rumor about Santa Claus. And he thought about that and he came home and he said, "Mom, I just want to ask... " Mother. He called her Mother. "I want to ask you straight out, and I want a straight answer. Is there a Santa Claus or isn't there?" And she said, "You asked for a straight answer, the answer is 'No', there isn't." And she was prepared for the disappointment and the tears and the frustration. He simply said, "S-s-h-h-e-e-w-w. I'm glad to hear that." And she said, "Why?" He said, "I would have been embarrassed the first Christmas after I got married to have my wife think I was looking for Santa Claus." (laughter) Hey, that's thinking for a first grader. His whole life he was thinking.

Dain was a philosopher. His graduate minor was in philosophy. He knew the philosophers and their philosophies. He was fascinated by the ability of the mind of man to think, to reason and to discover. John Wayne talked about the debates and discussions they had; we had them, too.

And I remember one time I asked him to make me a promise that he would always be intellectually honest, and he kept it.

Dain was somewhat of a multi-linguist, too. Not that he was conversant in many languages, but he could read several languages. He was fascinated by the study of words and languages: Russian, German, French Spanish, and he'd even dabbled in a little Japanese.

Pastor/Minister. Some of you may not be aware of that. Dain pastored a little church near Fowler, Indiana for a period of time.

Father. I am proud of the father Dain was. It was a dream fulfilled for him. You should have seen him when he came in from the University of Cincinnati at night. Uh, sometimes very late—as I speak to the department chair. (chuckle) You should have seen his face light up when those two little guys came running through the house with their arms outstretched, their faces lit up with joy.

One of the most memorable scenes about Dain and his fatherhood that comes to mind is... I went upstairs one evening and he was sitting at his computer up there just working as hard as he could work. And on his shoulders was one of the little guys—must have been about three or four months of age at the time—with a belt around the little guys' back and fastened around Dain's forehead (laughter). He's working on the computer while tears of joy were running down his cheeks. I'll never forget that scene. He was a good father.

And then another scene I like to remember is when he would sit at the piano and play some of the tunes he loved to play, and these two little guys sitting on the piano bench on either side of him just banging

away on the keys. Didn't bother Dain. He was just drifting across the keys in his own little world.

Professor/Teacher. This was his dream. This was his goal. This he worked for. And you may or may not know, he had opportunity to take much higher paying positions in industry, but he turned them down and moved to Cincinnati to do what he dreamed of and longed to do.

Son. My wife and I could tell you many stories

about what a great son Dain was. Dain and I shared a love for laughter. A great love for life. A great love for discussions.

And we had differences of opinion. Sometimes, major differences. But we always had deep honor and respect for one another. Most always on parting, and many times on being reunited, Dain and I kissed. You see, I loved my son.

He was a husband. And probably the most significant thing I can say about his ability to be a husband, was his ability to pick a wife.

I've talked a lot about his accomplishments and achievements, but you don't know about the odds and obstacles he had to overcome to get there; they were many: financial and physical. And his mother and I claim a lot of credit for the foundations that were laid, but I want to tell you something—I want all of you to know this—it was his wife Pat who enabled him. It was his wife Pat who urged him. It was his wife Pat who proved to be the wife that he thought she would be and pushed him on to achieve and accomplish and become.

Finally, I want to tell you this: He was a man. Decent, good, kind, gentle, hard working, creative, loving and intelligent.

Perfect?

No, because he took after his mother's side of the family. (laughter)

Joyce E. Samples, Dain's mother

(assisted by Dain's sister-in-law, Bobbi Samples.
After some coercion, Joyce joins Bobbi at the podium.)

Joyce: I have asked Bobbi to read what I wrote to say to you all today because I know I would never get it out.

Bobbi: It is my honor to read the words of this wonderful, gracious, loving lady...

To all our dear, dear family who have made that special effort to be here to pay tribute to our son, I say thank you for coming.

I thank you for your loving support during this most difficult time of our life; we are truly blessed by your presence.

We have been overwhelmed by your gracious outpouring of love and concern for us and yet why should we be so surprised when Christians do what Christians do best. I have chosen this way to express my feelings to my family, so please indulge me.

To my husband, John, my best friend, my counselor, and my lover, I say: We have traveled many miles together over the last 43 years, and that journey has not been without its rough rocky spots. So rough at times that it seemed impossible to continue, but our determination to preserve what is right and good has brought us to this day.

Today we walk the rockiest, and seemingly the most impassable road by far—we've lost our first-born son. For reasons we do not understand, we are left behind to ponder the events of the past four days. And, yes, we even question the untimely death of our son Dain, who gave us so much joy.

Today, we are faced with the biggest challenge of our life. That challenge requires that we keep on walking and that we walk straight and stand tall as we continue this journey of life.

Dain is a good example of tenacity and courage, so our tribute to him must be one of boldness and valor. So, keep walking, honey; I'm right by your side.

To my son, John Wayne: I say you, too, have been the source of much joy and happiness in my life. You have been given a challenge also. One that will be difficult to meet, and your hurt and anger will be hard to overcome. But because of your faith in God, and the wonderful memories you have with your brother, you will endure your loss, for God is with you each minute and each hour of every day. So, when you feel that life is unfair and too hurtful to bear, just reach out and touch the hand of the one that will sustain you in your grief.

To my sweet daughter, Bobbi: I say you are too precious to me.

BOBBI: I skipped over the words "daughter-in-law" not because I didn't see them, but because I have never felt such.

I wish for you all the happiness that you can glean from sharing your life with my son, John Wayne. Thank you for being a part of this family. You too will miss Dain. I know you will be sensitive to the needs of your little family as they mourn the loss of Dain.

To Shayne, my grandson: I pray that you will always be the sensitive person you are today, and I hope that you never experience so much hurt the rest of your life as you have seen the past four days, but if you do, may you handle it with the same spirit of love and affection as you have these past four hard days.

To my granddaughter, Mandi: What can I say to you except that I love you. You're a wonderful girl with a sweet, sweet spirit and a strong faith that will give you strength for the days ahead. Your Uncle Dain loved you and was happy that you are his namesake [Mandi Alain]. As you cope with his death, please wear his name proudly because he was proud of you.

To Galen and Ehren, my grand-twins: How sweet you are and oh how much pleasure you have given your daddy in the last fourteen months. Grandmother thinks you are the cutest pair she has ever seen and I find so much happiness in sharing your life.

But my greatest joy comes when I remember the words of your daddy when he said, "My life is fulfilled and my joy is complete because of my babies Galen and Ehren." Each day he would say, "I love them more than I did yesterday."

And he did. Your daddy died loving you more than life itself. Someday, my babies, you will understand what that kind of love means.

To my daughter-in-law, Pat: *<to my daughter Pat:>* There are no words that I can say that will take away the pain you feel this day. There is nothing I can do that can wipe away the fear you feel in your heart for the future. But I want to say to you before all these people that I love you because you loved my Dain. But I also love you for who you are, a woman of courage and determination to do the right thing. You can do it—God never turns his back on his children.

To my son Dain: How can I face tomorrow without you? For so many years we were miles and miles apart and had little opportunity to get to know each other well. Then after seventeen years you moved fifteen minutes away and I have enjoyed our times together so very much.

I discovered what a warm, tender, sensitive person you really were. I found so much joy in sharing your life with your little babies for whom you waited so long.

We have laughed and we have cried together and that created a bond between us that is so strong not even death can destroy.

But now you are gone and there is no way to describe the emptiness I feel inside. A part of me has died also.

But as your dad and I continue to walk this lonely road together, we will spot a rose every now and then that will remind us all over again that you are forever with us in spirit and memory -- and nobody can take that away from us.

Now, you have met your God, and you have met your Papa Daddy, and I'm confident that you have the answers to every question you have posed in the past years.

I love you, Son, and I'll love and help care for your sweet babies, telling them every day of your deep abiding love for them. So, now I say to you my sweet son—thank you for the wonderful memories.

Rose © 2013 by Ehren Samples

BOBBI: Those were Joyce's words. I can't speak for Dain, he's gone. But I can say without hesitation, that I know that Dain would be saying right here and now, not thanks to him, but thank you, Mom, for your unquestioning and undying love and devotion to him.

Patricia A. Samples, Dain's wife

I've been before many an audience, many a loving audience, but I don't think I've felt quite the love I feel here today.

Except from my husband, Dain Samples.

I didn't write down my remarks because I couldn't sit down for the last four days. Couldn't get off the phone because I couldn't stop answering it for myself.

Dain loved in a way I've yet to understand entirely, and your being here is a demonstration of that, and I thank you from the bottom of my heart, for your love and your appreciation of such a great man as my husband.

He loved his family, he loved life, he loved his sons, and his wife, and his friends, deeply.

He had a passion for thinking, and learning, and being, which is what led him to want and desire and work eight hard, torturous years to get there... to become an assistant professor at UC.

He was proud to be a colleague of many of you, and a teacher and a friend.

His greatest love was his students, his teaching.

We've made a memorial table to just begin to scratch the surface on the kind of person that Dain was. He was truly, in my opinion, a Renaissance man. One who cared and thought and looked at life and the world as something new to learn every single day.

Nothing bored him at all. He did carry a book with him at all times, and was never without a German dictionary, which he taught himself to speak.

I could go on forever, but I think I'll quit.

Thank you for everything.

For your on-going love and support.

For being here today, and being in our lives.

Devotional Thoughts
by Dr. Robert Shannon, Atlanta, Georgia
He and Dain's father shared in the conducting of
Dain & Pat's wedding January 1, 1972
in Largo, Florida.

Following the devotional,
further tributes were shared:

Dr. Vik J. Kapoor, ECE Department Chair, U of C

I speak today with great sorrow and sadness in my heart on behalf of the faculty, the technical, and the administrative staff, graduate students, as well as undergraduate-students of the University of Cincinnati where Dain Samples was a professor in the department of Electrical and Computer Engineering.

I talked to our president, Joe Steger, last night, and on behalf of the entire university, he sends his condolences and sympathy to the parents and the wife, and other relatives. So does Dean Papadakis, the dean of the college.

We were all stunned and speechless when we learned of the sudden passing away of our beloved friend, Dain Samples.

I met with him the previous Friday. We had a couple-hour chat. And we said, "Let's meet again next Wednesday,"—the day he passed away—because he will be gone for two days and I will have gone to Europe for three days.

I was informed as I landed at the Atlanta airport on Thursday at 4:30. And when my assistant informed me, I was really...

The Father, The Son, & The Brother's Ghost

The telephone fell out of my hand, and she has to start yelling, "Dr. Kapoor, are you still there?" It was so sudden.

I want to say with you, a few things. It very few times happens a faculty member gets very close to a department chair. (laughter) Because... I'm the reason given when they come home late. (laughter)

Two years ago at this time, we were interviewing him for the faculty position in our department. I distinctly remember, around 4:30, Professor Phil Wilsey, who is the Director of the computers program in our department, came running to me and he said, "Vik, Vik! We've got to hire this guy." I said, "What's big about this? We have interviewed 15 others," or about 12 at that time. He said, "Vik, our faculty feel not that he is only technically competent, who'll be an outstanding professor, but I'm telling you, he is going to make a difference!"

And I remember those words. And I want to share with you, how in last only... less than two years, he has made the difference!

I always felt his first love was for his teaching, and caring for his students. This year, for example, 10% of the senior class wanted to work with him to do their senior project. And when I informed them there were only two openings available, I nearly had a riot. (laughter)

I asked the students, "Why would you want to work with Professor Dain Samples? There are other 29 professors in the department." They say, "You know, Dr. Kapoor, he cares. He's going to make a difference, and we're going to get a better job."

And, knowing Dain, he took more students than normally a professor takes. Many, many more. And I have seen him spending his hours and days working with the students.

Professor Dain Samples was known to teach compiling; he was a computer scientist. He was in software. We hired him because he was the best in compiler computation theory. And he was the first such professor at the University of Cincinnati.

He built his own courses and program. These courses were never taught before.

At the end of the classes, we always have a teaching evaluation. Professors want to get feedback from the students. His teaching evaluations for all the two years—and I personally read all the evaluations of all the professors—his evaluations were between one and two. One is Excellent and Two is Very

Good. And it always was between one and two, better than any other professor in our department, consistently over a two year period.

He cares for his students, and that's what I meant, he made a difference.

He took on students... It was so sad... I reflect back, a few months back, one of his students' husband passed away and he and I went together to attend the memorial service.

Dain and I were close. As I said, that very rarely happens. He would be a person I could go to and seek advice.

I truly believe I lost a younger brother. He has been —now that I also know his wife Pat very well; his children; we have visited with Joyce and John at their house; enjoyed the children, when they got the twins. My children, I have twins, and enjoyed coming and visiting and sharing their experience with Dain and Pat.

Truly we lost a faculty member who's going to be very hard to replace and be very missed. In two years, he had made a mark on students, as you saw. So many students came here today to share.

At this time, I'd like to announce the formation—the department and the University of Cincinnati has decided to establish the:

Dain Samples Outstanding Senior Student Award.

It will be given every year to a senior because Dain was a faculty advisor to Eta Kappa Nu honor society. The plaque will be established and on the principles which Dain Samples stood for... We expect all his principles to be embodied in this award. It will be given every year, chosen by the faculty.

And again, in the end... I am grieved.

The department is grieved. We are stunned.

You have lost a best friend and a husband and a son and a brother.

We have lost also a brother.

May God rest his soul.

Dr. Harold Carter, Associate Professor
Dain's Mentor and Colleague

Dain was my friend.

It took only two years to obtain a friend that was one of the best. Within a university environment, often times the stresses and the activities become so demanding that it's hard for even relationships to develop any further than just sort of professionally or superficially. But with Dain, that didn't occur. It went deeper than that.

And not just for myself, but in talking with others in our department, Dain had an effect that was deeper than just a professional relationship. And so his passing was very deep to us.

I was by Dain's side within seconds after he'd collapsed; he found his way outside of the classroom, where his collapse occurred during the time he was doing what he enjoyed best; he was twenty minutes into a lecture he was giving that day.

He was teaching students that he dearly loved. He wanted to see their minds enriched. But more than that, he wanted to see the students develop as human beings. As people who are making a transition from youthfulness to professional to adulthood to maturity. So, his passing is doubly hard.

We had very brief conversations during the several minutes it took before the paramedics arrived. He realized the severity of his condition. And to the family—I, as many of you are, am a born-again Christian; very deep in my faith. I also have a son who has decided not to follow the ways he was raised in terms of his own spiritual growth. But remember, God's word does say, in Proverbs, that, train up a child in the way he should go, and when he is old, when he is mature, he will follow that way. And it is my belief that as a result of this understanding that Dain had in the last few moments of his life, that he had the opportunity to reflect on his childhood raising, and understand the importance of God within his life, and to perhaps at that time, accept Jesus Christ as his personal savior, and through that, clinch eternity with God our father.

So, in closing, I'd just like to state that Dain came to us, selected out of over 400 applicants; unanimous decision of the half-a-dozen computer science and engineering professors. We accepted him and immediately got to know him socially. I have fond memories of going with my son, with him and with Karen and Bobby Davis. I remember having a good time.

Then I remember being with Dain occasionally; remember receiving over E-Mail—we computer people tend to communicate a lot over E-Mail. He had sent to us after his first class that he taught, a two or three page explanation of how he perceived his course to have gone, the background work his students should have had in order to complete his course. At that moment, I think we as a faculty recognized that we had a person who not only would do the things that the time required, but would reflect back on them and let us know so that we all could improve.

He was severely demanding. But he did so because he wanted to see others reach their potential.

So, let me just say that, he was my friend, and I'm going to miss him.

John C. Samples

This was Dain's Day. Thank all of you who made it possible.

So many people to thank for so many things. I have a friend here who drove all the way from Nashville, Tennessee just, willingly brought the sound equipment for us; Ron Worrell, and I appreciate that so much.

People have driven from Florida, Georgia, Pennsylvania, Nebraska (chuckle); our younger son was in Nebraska when the news came.

I think Dain's Day has been just right. Thank you Dr. Shannon for your just right words.

Thank all of you for your presence.

We're not going to leave if someone else has something they want to add. Please, come to the microphone.

Anyone else... Collect your thoughts. Dr. Shannon has to leave to catch a plane.

I don't know if anybody else has to leave or not, but this is Dain's Day and... I don't know if you met Puddy Bear or not, but... this little Teddy Bear here has been with Dain since about two years of age. He took it to college with him. (laughter) He was there when he got his Ph.D.

It's interesting how we learn to love what those we love love. Ever notice that?

Other students, friends, and family members may share their thoughts and feelings at this time.

Nasir Abbas, one of Dain's students

I can't say much to you all, but I would like to say a few things to Dr. Samples. I'm sure he's here.

I never got a chance to say anything when he was with us, so I'd just like to take this opportunity to say, he was my advisor. Not only in my academics, but in all my matters that troubled me. I could go to him, turn to him, and speak to him about anything that I wanted.

Dr. Samples was a very patient person. I am not a very good student. I know for a fact, I am not very good student. There are much, much better students than I am. He was very tolerant with me. He taught me whatever I had curiosity about. He always cleared-up everything for me; many times. He never told me I was wrong; he always wanted me to search for the answer, if I was wrong. He never said, "You are wrong," or "This idea won't work." He gave me an opportunity to find it out for myself. That way, I grew into a better person in the last two years of my masters program.

Comparing him to the other professors, he was extremely tolerant. I mean, I would become impatient with him (laughter), really. He was so tolerant with every student. I was one of his research students and we had questions and he would be answering questions of his class students. With so much patience... I never saw it in any person.

And he used to explain each and every step. He never wanted anyone to fail in his class or get a bad grade. He cared about the students so much. It's very tough on all of us; he was a very good friend to all of us.

I really don't have too many words to say for him. He was really a great person. In my heart... the place I have for him... it cannot be replaced by anybody else. He is really irreplaceable in all aspects.

On behalf of all the students in our research group, I'd like to convey our condolences to you all, to the family and relatives of Dr. Samples. And we just want you to have courage.

It is very difficult on all of us, but I guess he is the lucky one; he got out of all the miseries of this life. He escaped all of it, so he is really the lucky one.

Thank you for the opportunity.

Terry Craft, Dain's Sister-in-law

Extemporaneously and off the top of my head, this could be hard to do.

My brother-in-law was a very unique individual, and, I didn't have a lot of years to spend close to him, because they did live in California for a long time. But we had many a debate, even over the telephone (laughter). I think three things remind me of Dain, or come to me when I think of Dain. One of them is the word "wonder". Dain seemed to always wonder.

We've heard that kind of said here today; John Wayne reflected on the fact that Dain was always questioning, debating, and from that he learned.

Anything that happened—with the boys in the last year particularly—it's been so fun to watch him when he was around us, that everything was a wonder that his little boys did and he just couldn't...

I know we've probably all done it with our kids, every little thing that they did he was always looking at the educational value of whatever that was, or how it was going to affect them, or what they would do with that in the future, you know, how that would be.

The other word I think that comes to me when I think of Dain is the word joy. He really was a fun person, most all the time, to be with. I know with his students he was probably serious, but I betcha there were plenty of times when there were fun things in what he did or what he said or how he told you to do something. I know he's always been that way with family and friends.

On the memory table, if you'll look around you'll see that a lot of the things we were able to pull out and pull from Dain were joke books, and notes on his table. Little quips and quotes that he had put here and there. I think one of them, or a couple of them, are shared in your bulletin today.

And one last thing that he really always did, and that was the questioning. The questioning of the hereafter; the questioning of life in general. And, to me anyway, it always seems that, somehow, that when we get into education, education in itself sometimes can give us a lot more questions than it gives us answers. And he really always was searching, and I really believe that at this point, he's found his answers. I hope that all of you will take that as some kind of a lesson for each one of you.

If we don't gain anything else from the life that we

shared in those years with Dain, I think that's one thing that we should know; that questioning is good, searching is wonderful; education is great, but at some point you have to stop and try to take in to your own inner faith, your own inner feelings, and your own inner needs, and know what they are.

In Dain's own way, he kind of preached his own ministry over the years. He started out as a minister a long time ago, and I sat in church a couple of times and listened to him preach as a preacher, and he was good. He didn't like that as well as he did teaching, but he was good at it, as I'm sure he would've been at almost anything he'd undertaken to do. But I think that that's kind of the ministry he's given; teaching us all to search just a little bit. Soul search. Book search. Whatever it takes to come up with the faith that you need to get on in this life, and Dain's found his now. Thank you.

Charlie Farnum, Dain's former officemate at the University of California at Berkeley

I wasn't with him all of those eight years (laughter), I was with him for five. I would certainly echo the statements about his love, and his concern, and his searching for truth. But, there's one thing I think he would want his students to know... I presume he told his wife and parents at some point, but, one of the reasons it took him eight year's to do it [get his Ph.D.], was... he would insist time and again that he wasn't going to let the university get in the way of his education. (laughter)

And I encourage you not to let that happen either. There are regulations and things you have to do, but he... If something came up that he had to learn about, whether it was philosophy or German, or some part of computer science that wasn't going to count toward his degree, he would look at it and learn about it.

I didn't have his wisdom of years, I guess, and so I got out a little bit earlier.

I also had family back home to come to, and, the last thing I guess... We both were sort of in this situation of being out on the west coast and wanting to come back home. That was part of his dream and part of mine. I came back home and was with my mother for a year, and then she died. And it hurt then tremendously, and it still hurts a lot. But the year was good. It was good to get back home and be there for that time to have back together again.

And I'm sure, that for Dain, it was also good to get back home and have that time together.

John C. Samples

That prompts an observation that I wanted to comment on earlier and neglected to.

The question comes that, Dain worked so hard and sacrificed so much to achieve the goals that were important to him, and then didn't have time to enjoy them.

But the point is, he accomplished them!

I think that's the real point. Press on. Press on.

Roxanna Redick, Dain's Cousin

This is no easier for me than any of the other family.

Dain and I were about three months apart; they used to put us in the same crib together when we were tiny. Most of you knew him as a grown man; I knew him as a child, and all the things that have been said about him as an adult were true as a child.

We explored things together. We looked for things together. We even had children together as we [my husband Bruce and I] have a daughter who is fourteen months old, as his twins are. Yet, the one thing I remember about him most is the day he held her, and he looked at me and said, "It answers the question; not all babies are the same. Those (the twins) are mine, and she's wonderful."

He knew... When those little boys came, Pat, when you two were a complete family... you were always together, but that finished out everything he'd ever wanted. You completed a dream he had, even as a child, that what he knew had to go to someone else.

Thank you all for learning from him.

Steve Roberts, Dain's roommate at Milligan

Steve's closing remarks and prayer
were not recorded.

The service lasted 95 minutes, the tape lasted 90.

Like Dain, the tape did not last long enough for us.

The End

Shadow On The Stage

Shadow On The Stage

The music has stopped, the curtain is drawn,
the last line is now delivered.

The words of the play, the soul of his song,
continue to be considered.

The Actor was good, he pulled us all in,
his success is easy to gauge.

Is he still there? Be still and listen,
for the shadow up on the stage.

I tried to do it, to be just like him,
this Actor I so admired.

He helped me along, through bright lights and dim,
And always kept me inspired.

The roles got tougher, we were not lacking,
we both were now earning our wage.

He was an actor, I was just acting,
Like the shadow, now on the stage.

To share with others, he turned to teaching,
to helping those who sought him out.

To learn for himself, he turned to reaching,
and seeking to answer his doubts.

I watched from afar, this tutor of mine,
he learned every word on his page.

We walked far apart, but always in rhyme,
that shadow, and me, on the stage.

The scene is not through, his role not complete,
when the Producer calls his name.

The patrons scream "Foul", for none can compete,
the play, it just won't be the same.

His first student knows, though tries not to say,
the questions, the pain and the rage.

The Actor left this, when he went away:
left me, his shadow, on the stage.

What will we do now? The Actor is gone.
Will someone move into his place?

Can someone be found, to go it alone?
Will 1 fight his fight, run his race?

The answer is "No", for it will take 2:
Those students the youngest in age.

His first pupil smiles, now slightly off cue,
at three shadows left on the stage.

John Wayne Samples
April, 1993

Postscript

So far, this little book—this tribute to my brother—has been about us; our sorrows and our celebrations, our wonderings and our wanderings.

But what would Dain have to say?

I could guess, but I would be wrong.

It seems appropriate that we finish this reflection with his own words; something that we know he considered to be a significant accomplishment, from the world in which he endeavored to make a difference.

Almost exactly two years before he died, Dain finished his Ph.D. dissertation entitled:

Profile-Driven Compilation.

The entire document was more than 180 pages long, single-spaced. We'll settle here for the *abstract*, the *conclusion*, the *summary* and his *acknowledgments*. That's more than most of us can understand about it, anyway.

I have done my best to proof Dr. Dain's writing for accuracy. If you understand these things enough to have an opinion on the technical information herein, feel free to let me know of any typographical corrections. If you think the work is wrong, take it up with a computer.

And one last note. As I was completing this project I did a search on the Internet to see what might turn up under the name of Dain Samples; our father and I do that from time to time. Twenty years gone from an industry that seems to change every twenty days and his work continues to be cited by peers and students alike. In the past twelve months alone his work has been registered on web sites that track such things as having been referenced in at least ten new publications and academic writings in the computer and engineering fields.

Remarkable.

Yes he was.

Profile-Driven Compilation

by Alan Dain Samples

Abstract

As the size and complexity of software continues to grow, it will be necessary for software construction systems to collect, maintain, and utilize much more information about programs than systems do now. This dissertation explores compiler utilization of profile data.

Several widely held assumptions about collecting profile data are not true. It is not true that the optimal instrumentation problem has been solved, and it is not true that counting traversals of the arcs of a program flow graph is more expensive and complex than counting executions of basic blocks. There are simple program flow graphs for which finding optimal instrumentations is possibly exponential. An algorithm is presented that computes instrumentations of a program to count arc traversals (and therefore basic block counts also). Such instrumentations impose 10% to 20% overhead on the execution of a program, often less than the overhead required for collecting basic block execution counts.

An algorithm called Greedy Sewing improves the behavior of programs on machines with instruction caches. By moving basic blocks physically closer together if they are executed close together in time, miss rates in instruction caches can be reduced up to 50%. Arc-count profile data not only allows the compiler to know which basic blocks to move closer together, it also allows those situations that will have little or no effect on the final performance of the reorganized program to be ignored. Such a low-level compiler optimization would be difficult to do without arc-count profile data.

The primary contribution of this work is the development of TypeSetter, a programming system that utilizes profile data to select implementations of program abstractions. The system integrates the development, evaluation, and selection of alternative implementations of programming abstractions into a package that is transparent to the programmer. Unlike previous systems, TypeSetter does not require programmers to know details of the compiler implementation. Experience indicates that the TypeSetter approach to system synthesis has considerable benefit, and will continue to be a promising avenue of research.

[The other 176 pages of the dissertation would go here]

Conclusion

For the last twenty years, no one has agreed with Knuth's Dictum (see page 1) enough to implement the idea, nor has anyone proven the assertion false. There are several assumptions in the Dictum, two of which have formed the central hypotheses of this work. They are:

that profiling can be done efficiently enough so as not to be perceived as onerous by the programmer; and,

that compilers and other tools can automatically extract useful information from profile data.

In the process of investigating the first of these

hypotheses, I determined that an implicit assumption held by many programmers is false. Most programmers (myself included) have believed that counting executions of basic blocks is sufficient and more efficient than getting the more complete information about arc traversals. I demonstrated in Chapter 2 that this simply is not so. I presented an algorithm MINOPT which finds the 'optimal' instrumentation of a program by automatically placing the instrumentation code in the nodes or on the arcs. Previous algorithms have found optimal solutions for nodes, or for arcs. MINOPT is the first provably minimal algorithm for both nodes and arcs. I also pointed out that the 'optimal' algorithms aren't, that all have assumed the ability to compute instrumentation costs in linear time. I do not know whether there exists such an algorithm or not, but I have shown that if it does exist, it cannot be 'local'. That is, when estimating the instrumentation costs of a node's incoming and outgoing arcs, more information is required than just the execution frequencies of that node and its arcs.

My measurements showed that profiling in the form of in-line execution counts imposes anywhere from 10% to 20% overhead. This can be predicted solely from the observation that most programs' basic blocks average from four to ten instructions in size, and from the not to o unrealistic assumption that incrementing a counter in memory requires ab out the average number of cycles for the execution of an instruction on a machine. Therefore, putting instrumentation in the most frequently executed basic block will produce a slowdown of 10-20% for the program as a whole.

Programmers would complain if a programs were slowed down 10-20% for no reason. That is, if no one (or thing) was making any use of the profile data, then programmers would turn off profile collection. (That is why all compilers today require the programmer to specify when to collect profile data.) However, the second of the hypotheses above would alleviate the problem considerably. If some part of the programming system were able to utilize the profile data to produce superior programs, then the profile collecting overhead is not onerous. It is comparable to the overhead of non-optimized bounds-checking code. While there has been some research in improving the overhead of profile collection (in particular, see Sarkar's paper on using dependency graphs to optimize profile counting [42]), there has yet to be a definitive exploration of the optimization of profile counting.

For there to be such research, it has to be shown that continual collection of profile data is a win. Therefore, I concentrated in Chapters 3 and 4 in exploring ways a compiler might make use of profile data. In Chapter 3 I presented an algorithm I call Greedy Sewing for improving the behavior of programs on machines with instruction caches. By physically moving basic blocks closer together that are executed close together in time, miss rates in instruction caches can be reduced up to 50%. Profile data not only allows the compiler to know which basic blocks to move closer together, it also allows it to ignore those situations where it will not matter to the final performance of the program.

The primary contribution of this work is the development of a program- ming system that utilizes profile data to select implementations of program abstractions. The TypeSetter system integrates the development, evaluation, and selection of alternative implementations of programming abstractions into a package that is transparent to the User. Unlike previous systems, TypeSetter does not require specialized compiler knowledge of the User or the Implementor. From the data collected so far, the TypeSetter approach to system synthesis app ears to be a promising avenue of research.

Problems and future work

I have only scratched the surface of the body of engineering problems that need to be solved before TypeSetter can be considered a complete system. Some of these are related to problems inherent in using profile data to predict the future performance of a program, but others are related to the specific approach taken by TypeSetter.

Execution counts: During this work, I fell into an assumption that I think is widely shared, but which can cause problems. I had assumed that summing profile counts across multiple runs of a program was a reasonable approach to understanding the behavior of a program. But consider a program that has a function that is called once for each element on a list. For 99% of the elements, the function requires O (1) time to execute. But for 1 out of 100 elements, it requires much more time. For example, let us assume that the occurrence of a certain kind of element requires that it be put in a separate list, and that sorting this list n-element list requires O (n2) time (it uses an inefficient sorting algorithm) where n = 1. If the program is run M times, and the profile counts used as measures of the complexity of this function are summed, then there comes a point where the one-in-a-hundred event dominates the analysis. If we assume a list that is 100 elements long, and one of the elements causes a re-sort, then running the program 100 times could make the list look like it was 10,000 elements long, with 100 re-sorts, implying that the sorting of the special elements requires as much time as the processing of the non-special elements, when in fact it never sorts a list longer than one element.

In general, this problem will rear its head when evaluation functions are non-linear in the values of the profile variable. For profilers like *prof* and *gprof*, this may not cause any particular problem, even though their output does not indicate how many runs of the program produced the data on which they base their analysis. Therblig was modified to count the number of executions of a program in addition to the counters specified in the profiling implementations. During analysis, all counters were divided by the number of program runs to try to avoid problems similar to the ones described in the previous paragraph. However, I am not satisfied that this avoids all problems of analysis from execution counts derived from multiple runs. This needs to be examined further.

Evaluation functions: The most difficult functions to write in TypeSetter are the evaluation functions. While some of the difficulty is due to the fact that I've never had to write functions that evaluate the potential performance of other functions in such numbers before, they bring their own set of problems. For one thing, they are hardly ever 'wrong', at least not in the sense that inaccuracies produce obviously aberrant behavior on the part of the program. I have serendipitously discovered several instances where evaluation expressions I have written do not accurately reflect the performance of the actual function; even ignoring the fact that these are all estimates anyway, the results returned were misleading. Debugging these routines to a reasonable level of accuracy is difficult.

Kenny and Lin [27] report a technique for capturing the behavior of functions that might be usable in a Therblig-like environment. The Implementor would specify an expression with free variables that he suspects would adequately capture the behavior of the function in question; for example, $A*x+B*y^2+C$, where x and y are parameters such as the length of a list, or size of set. By executing the function many times on many inputs, an average behavior for the function based on x and y can be found by determining appropriate values for A, B and C with a curve fitting algorithm. While this may be an approach for rigorously and more automatically producing evaluation functions, it will not reduce the amount of work required by the Implementor and may impede the Implementor from taking advantage of logical information contained in the profile data. For example, a curve-fitting approach may not be able to handle knowledge about the density of bit vectors, order of presentation of elements to a function, etc.

In general, evaluation functions need to be easier to write and debug.

Evaluating ADT-invoked User functions: There are several optionals that require the names of User-defined functions. The ones I have identified are ObjToInt, IntToObj, and compareFcn. They present problems when used because TypeSetter has no way of estimating the runtime resources of the indicated functions. Presumably, future systems will have the User give some indication of the cost of executing these functions so that the evaluation functions can give better estimates of the cost of using implementations that require them. I would like to avoid forcing the User to write evaluation functions: that is mixing the roles of User and Implementor to o much. Exactly how to achieve the same result without User-written evaluation routines is yet to be determined.

The prototype finesses the problem entirely. Currently, the Ob jToInt function must always be a reference to an integer field of the object, and IntToObj must be an array reference. This has not been terribly restrictive up to this point, but since the maintenance of the array of objects must be done by the User, it imposes some overhead that should be eliminated. Ideally, a map from integers to objects, and its inverse, should not be in the final implementation of a program unless it is needed. Currently, it will always be there, whether Therblig selects implementations that use them or not.

Second-order effects: Another problem arises when there are dependencies in the User program that are not part of the information available to a Therblig-like analyzer. Consider a program that keeps objects sorted on a list, but has its own sorted-list code rather than using a library routine. The list is created from a set of these objects, the implementation of said set assigned by the system. It could turn out that the implementation of the set causes the elements to be returned in an order that interferes with the efficient execution of the User's code: i.e. one implementation of set returns the elements in the order of their memory address which corresponds to the order in which they were constructed which in turn corresponds to the order data was read from a file. It is easy to see that there could be interference between the User's implementation and any implementation chosen by the system for the set, and no amount of analysis of the User's use of the set would uncover it.

This is outside the scope of a Therblig style system. One of its major premises is that looking at the use of the ADTs alone is sufficient to make a reasonable assignment, and extra-ADT information is simply not made available to it. I have not encountered this kind of second-order effect in any of the programs I have run through Therblig, but theoretically it is possible.

Implementation containment: When a bit vector implementation of a set of size N is instantiated, then any declaration of a smaller set could share the code for the larger set. This would decrease the program's memory size further, at the expense of making the space allocated for some sets larger. Discovering and taking advantage of these tradeoffs would require the evaluation functions to consider space as well as time in their analysis. Since Low, for one, has already considered the more complex space-and-time integral objective function for minimization, I felt that duplicating this was not necessary to my objectives and I have concentrated on the simpler time-analysis.

Even if Therblig were capable of handling the space analysis, there is nothing in its analysis framework that would allow the kinds of implementation containment described above. In other words, there is no way for the evaluation functions written by the Implementor to conclude "Use implementation X unless condition Y holds, in which case use implementation Z." Again, future work will have to show, first, that this is an optimization that needs to be available and, second, how to obtain it.

Design of implementation libraries: I have barely begun to explore the possibilities in a library of implementations. As mentioned before, it may be desirable to have several profiling implementations, each capable of collecting certain kinds of information that is otherwise difficult to obtain. For example, once a bit vector implementation of a set is determined to be desirable, another bit-vector oriented profiling implementation could be used to determine which of the many bit vector implementations would be best for this program.

In the interests of simplicity, I have also avoided making use of the more complex language features available in my base language, C++. For instance, the implementations List_slist, Set_slist, and Map_slist all use the same implementations of a linked list as their underlying representation. Currently, they each have their own copies of this code, primarily because the kinds of profiling information collected differs between the implementations. It is possible that they could all be derived from a linked-list class, increasing even further the possibilities for code sharing. Future work is needed to look at integrating the class hierarchy and attendant inheritance into the library of implementations.

Summary

I have explored in some detail the proposition that compilers and language systems can make use of profile data in the generation of code for programs, and in the synthesis of large software systems. I have improved the existing 'optimal' instrumentation algorithms, and shown how arc counts can be used to improve the execution time of programs on machines with instruction caches. I have presented the design of a language and attendant system that can select for a User the implementations of variables declared to be of an abstract data type. I have also demonstrated that such a system can make reasonable choices for those implementations based on the profile data collected by abstraction-specific profiling implementations.

Acknowledgements

My heartfelt appreciation goes first and foremost to my wife Pat for being patient (almost) every time I reported that I needed just six more months, nine at the most. That she could continue to be encouraging and excited about my work is almost more than I can understand. This dissertation is dedicated to her.

Whatever I have accomplished, it is because I have stood on the shoulders of two of the most loving giants I shall ever know. My dreams could not even have been dreamt without the many accomplishments achieved by my parents. I simply cannot find the words that sufficiently express my thanks and admiration.

I am grateful to Bruce MacLennan for more than he can possibly know. I thank him most for his friendship, his intellect, and encouragement. A lot of him, Gail, and Kimmie are in these pages. Thank you.

I may never have started on this task without the inspiration and downright prodding (goading?) of Dick Hamming and his perspective on the true meaning of a Ph.D.

"[W]e greatly appreciated the valuable suggestions by ... Sue Graham, ... And, especially, Paul Hilfinger — the reviewers who provided most of the comments that kept us busy for so long producing the final draft." [13] I am particularly pleased that I never had to make use of Paul's dimes. I also thank Stuart Dreyfus for his work on my thesis committee.

If I acknowledged everyone the way I want to, these acknowledgements could easily become longer than the dissertation itself. Therefore, I hope a simple thanks suffices for everyone who has helped me achieve this goal. Special thanks to Dr. Rodney Farrow, the unofficial fourth member of my committee, and to Dr. Wendy Sinclair-Brown for helping me see early on what was really important; thanks to Michelle and Allen for their valuable friendship; to Dave Ungar, Richard Probst, and other members of the Stiletto Club; to Eduardo and Vicki; to Michael and Karen; to Charlie and Kendall; to Doug; and especially to Toni, Mara, and everyone in 508-20 for putting up with me and helping me during the Final Days.

This dissertation was supported in part by an AT&T Bell Laboratories Scholarship, and by the Defense Advanced Research Projects Agency (DoD), monitored by Space and Naval Warfare Systems Command under Contract N00039-88-C-0292. Their support is very gratefully acknowledged.

-Alan Dain Samples
April, 1991

Dain & John Wayne, 1969